THE LITTLE
BLACK BOOK
OF SUPERVISION

THE LITTLE
BLACK BOOK
OF SUPERVISION

GIL SARGENT

Edited by Lois Sargent.

Copyright © 2003 by Gil Sargent.

ISBN :   Hardcover   1-4134-1295-5
            Softcover   1-4134-1294-7

This book was printed in the United States of America.

The Journey to Effective Supervision—Second Edition training workbook, Copyright ã 2002 by Gil Sargent

The Journey to Effective Supervision—First Edition training workbook, Copyright ã 2000 by Gil Sargent

Additional copies of this book, on-site management training or maintenance management consulting services may be requested from **THE CENTER FOR ADVANCED MANAGEMENT**™ To inquire e-mail us at *cenadvman@elko.net* or call 775-753-6092.

To order additional copies of this book, contact:
Xlibris Corporation
1-888-795-4274
www.Xlibris.com
Orders@Xlibris.com
19333

CONTENTS

Foreword

by Scott Santti

In 1994, I had an opportunity to oversee the startup and production of underground mining operations for one of the largest gold-producing companies in the world. [1] We had many open pit mines at the time, but no underground mines, and while some people in the corporation would rather have focused on the potentials for failure in this seemingly uncertain endeavor, a few of us looked at it as a new opportunity with tremendous future potential.

Yet to be successful at starting something new or at changing existing paradigms, it requires good team players, a lot of teamwork and a great deal of dedication and hard work. I wish I could say that I had recognized at the time the exact type of person required to ensure success in this new venture, but I didn't. I did recognize, however, that it would take a tremendous team effort. Teams win and are successful; individuals, left on their own, will never be as successful.

During the first year of construction and startup of the new mines, Gil Sargent was a member of our team as a front-line supervisor. As manager of the project, I saw that something about him was different. He stood out. He stood out because he was sincere, honest, hardworking, humble, skilled in his trade, organized in his work, and seemed to have the ability to communicate well with all levels within the organization.

As our hunch about this new opportunity proved correct, and underground mining expanded within the organization, the team made some incredible progress, and the author's skills and team efforts continued to contribute to the success of the company's bottom line, as well as benefiting him personally.

These are a few of the traits that Gil possesses that made him stand out.

- Organized—Determining who needs to accomplish what critical tasks and by when.
- Great communicator—Teaching and training expectations through both verbal and written methods with all levels (direct reports, peers and bosses).
- Hardworking—Sets the example.
- Positive attitude—Always smiling.
- Trained his people—Ensured they had the skills to do the job.
- Listened—Ensured his understanding of what people were telling him.
- Accountability—Fair, yet firm, to the people who reported to him.
- Continuous improvement—Always strived for the efficient and effective use of labor, supplies, equipment, tools, etc.

Gil Sargent knows the importance of both good management and leadership, and continually strives to learn more, while working to help others improve their skills as well. This book shares a complete list of the skills required and desired to help you become a successful supervisor. The author's experience and knowledge have captured them well.

My advice to the reader is to be receptive, learn and remember what is written in this book. Learning the skills and traits in this book will pay future dividends in your career as a business leader.

On a personal note, I will forever be appreciative of his help, which contributed greatly to my own success.

Scott Santti graduated from Michigan Tech in 1979 with a Bachelor of Science in Mine Engineering. Over the course of twenty-four years working in mining, he has been promoted through the ranks from mine engineer, to surface mine general foreman, surface mine superintendent, underground mine manager, and in early 2003, mine general manager. He is known for his ability to successfully organize and complete large projects, and his skills as a leader have helped many strive to reach their full potential.

Introduction

Those who work in jobs that are critically important are required to have extensive training before they can begin working solo. Doctors, lawyers, engineers, even plumbers are required to complete rigorous training before entering the workforce on their own.

So how is it that those who have a role of such crucial importance in business—that of supervisor—are not required to have the appropriate training? As it is, not only is such training not required, it is rarely available.

I ran my first crew while still working as an electrical apprentice in Wyoming. I've since worked my way up to superintendent, having had responsibility for over 250 employees, yet it was during those first years when I worked with journeyman electricians and electrical foremen that I began learning many of the skills I would later use a department head.

From my earliest experiences as a journeyman electrician, I learned how important it is to work hard and apply yourself, using both your head and your hands, so the job comes in on time and under budget. I learned that the fundamental role of the supervisor is to provide the tools, materials and equipment needed to get the job done. When that is done, a good supervisor gets out of the way and lets his employees do their job.

Yet, I knew I was still missing something. I understood that while most people do their fair share of the work, there are always a few who prefer skating through, never really earning their pay. On small jobs, with small crews, it was easy to see who was doing the work and who was not. Even though I understood it is the supervisor's job to motivate ineffective employees, many times I didn't do enough. The reason? I did not have the proper training and strategy to help my employees to become more efficient, and so I simply worked around the problem.

As I began moving up the ladder—from a journeyman running jobs, to front-line supervisor, to general foreman, to superintendent—I began to better understand the tremendous impact these unproductive employees, and their supervisors, have on profitability and their own chance to be associated with a winning company. I learned that as the number of employees I was responsible for grew, my responsibility for improving individual productivity also grew.

Looking back on it now, however, it's clear that had I received the same quality training and preparation in becoming a supervisor that I received in becoming an electrician, I would have been much more effective, much earlier.

The mission of this book is to provide insight into supervising for those who have been promoted into one of the most difficult jobs a person can take on. The information found in these pages is not typically taught in colleges or in trade schools. The information contained herein comes from twenty-five years of being in industry, and learning from some very good supervisors, as well as from very poor ones. It comes from struggling as an inexperienced new supervisor, through building the experience necessary to become a seasoned and effective supervisor. It comes from understanding that you don't have to learn it all on your own. Reach out to others who are willing to teach the critical lessons that will help you avoid the mistakes you otherwise might make.

This book is intended for those who supervise, whether they are department heads in a big company, the foreman on a crew, or a shift manager in a small business. It is intended to help you become effective faster, by giving you insight into the profession that many are forced to learn by trial and error over the course of several years. It is intended to help you understand that working hard, the thing you were probably promoted for, is not enough. To be effective you must learn how to multiply your impact by instilling in your employees a strong work ethic.

I had two reasons for writing this book. First, I hope to repay those who so generously shared their skills with me, by passing them along to the next generation of supervisors. Second, I wrote this book for supervisors who are looking for information that will help them supervise crews and manage companies successfully. I hope that by sharing my experiences, and referencing the insightful work of others, supervisors will be better prepared to handle the challenges they will face everyday.

Stop! Don't Waste Your Time

Who wants to work hard only to feel their effort is wasted? That's why I insist in my management training classes that my students sign an "Effort to Improve" contract. I do this to try to ensure that each student return to the job and exert the effort necessary to influence change and improve performance. If students are not serious about improving their skills, attending management classes is a waste of their time, their company's time, and my time.

As I ask this of my management students, I would also like to ask each of you, the readers, to do the same. Please decide now if you plan to work to improve your performance, and to positively influence the performance of others around you. If not, you should put this book down and do something more worthwhile with your time.

Chapter 1

Effective Supervision

The Supervisor's Circle of Skills

The success of any company is dependent upon, and limited by, the leadership and management skills of the supervisors of that company. This invisible boundary, which provides support for, yet ultimately limits employee and company performance, is called the Supervisor's Circle of Skills. The Circle of Skills is similar to the invisible field of gravity that holds everything close to earth. Gravity serves us well—up to a point. It is only when people are able to see the possibilities beyond this boundary, such as manned space flight, that the limiting aspects of gravity become clear.

In the same way, the Supervisor's Circle of Skills provides a positive influence for companies, especially in large companies composed of disparate groups of workers. It gives cohesion to the work force. It centers and supports employees and provides structure for individuals working to achieve company goals. It serves companies well, up to a point. However, just as gravity is limiting, so too are our leadership and management skills. As you might expect, when supervisors see new possibilities, and strive to expand their own Circle of Skills by learning additional techniques and strategies, they are likely to feel the pull of their own comfort levels. If they succeed, however, and their efforts prove rewarding, current management boundaries will be pushed toward new frontiers of improved employee performance, and by direct correlation, improved company performance.

The Supervisor's Circle of Skills

Figure 1

A simple example can be given in a production setting. If an employee is given a task, which by all historical account is known to be a two-hour task, yet your management team has an inefficient planning system in place that forces the employee to look for tools and parts for 20 minutes, putting the completion of the job at two hours and twenty minutes, then that is the fastest the employee will ever complete that job, regardless of how talented the employee is or how hard he tries to complete the job quickly.

Yet some will question "But it's only twenty minutes?" When considered for a task that is repeated thousands of times a year, however, the impact in lost productivity is substantial.

Thus, employee performance is limited by the boundary of management's vision of what is an acceptable Circle of Skills for their supervisors. No matter how good our employees are, supervisors with inadequate skills will limit their ability to perform to their potential. If employees perform poorly, management is responsible. If companies want to improve, they must enlarge and enhance the skills of their supervisors.

This daunting responsibility, once understood, might make new supervisors wish they could return to the plant floor and become just one of the workers again. Yet, those promoted to supervision are there because they are not easily discouraged or dissuaded.

The job of supervisor is one of the hardest of all management jobs, wielding more direct control over company success than any other position in the company.

Front-line supervisors and middle managers are in a pressure cooker. They are sandwiched between the unrelenting expectations of upper management and the unforgiving expectations of the employees whom they supervise. This book is intended to help you survive this pressure by supplementing your skills, bolstering your confidence, and increasing your chance for success.

Let's start with the two core skill components of supervising people, leading and managing.

The first major skill component of supervision is that of manager. The supervisor is responsible for managing the company's resources: employee time, materials, tools, machinery and equipment, to insure the maximum benefit is received from each. Managing involves setting targets, performance standards and completion schedules, and then building a set of measures to continually monitor progress.

Most supervisors are more comfortable in the manager role. The manager uses tangible and more easily understood tools including time measurement and performance statistics. Effective managers **MEASURE** performance to insure acceptable levels are maintained.

The second major skill component of supervision is that of leader. Leaders must have the ability to inspire and motivate those around them to performance levels greater than those achieved in the past. Leadership skills may come naturally to a few but most supervisors must learn and develop these skills. Leadership skills include the use of your voice, your physical presence, your understanding of people and your ability to motivate through inspirational communication. Effective leaders **INSPIRE** employees to perform at the highest possible levels.

The following are the leadership and managerial skills that makeup the Supervisor's Circle of Skills, and that companies look for when promoting employees to supervisor: [2]

The Manager's Skills

Organizational Ability—The ability to organize the

resources in your charge: employee time, equipment, tools and materials. Managers build control systems that insure a minimum level of performance, which includes goal-setting systems based on the principle, "What gets measured gets done." [3]

Administrative Skills—Supervisors must have the ability to handle the administrative duties that go with any management job. The inability to deal with administrative functions leads to losing track of employee time, job tools and materials, and results in inefficiencies, waste and added costs.

Mechanical Skill—Supervisors that have comparable skills with their employees are better able to relate to those employees because the employee feels more comfortable taking orders from someone whose skills they can respect. Good mechanical skills make it easier for the employee to accept the supervisor's judgment of their work.

Technical Skill—The modern supervisor must be able to deal with computerized material management and data entry systems, engineering drawings, specifications and mechanical instruction.

Education—This includes informal education, including past work experiences, the ability to understand the work at hand, the ability to read, understand and carry out company policies and procedures, and the understanding and willingness to ask for help when they need it.

The Leader's Skills

Motivational Skills—Your ability to lead employees to turn out satisfactory work because they want to, not because they have to. This includes the ability to clearly communicate expectations and inspire employees to get results.

Decision-Making Skills—Not every situation a supervisor will encounter can be solved with a policy or procedure. The supervisor must have good judgment and the ability to make quick decisions.

Initiative—Supervisors who don't lead by setting an example of energy and enthusiasm shouldn't expect their employees to be hard charging and energetic. Effective supervisors understand it is their job to set the example for everyone else.

Character—Supervisors have got to be straight shooters to gain the respect of their employees. If they're not, they arouse distrust and suspicion, not only about themselves but also about the company.

Human Interest—Supervisors should be aware of the things that affect the attitude of their employees. An employee's attitude can affect their job performance. Rarely can you do more than listen but rarely does it take more than that.

The Spheres of Influence

Supervisors step into the roles of manager and leader to interact with other employees in two completely different ways. The manager has authority over those below them in their direct reporting line. Leaders, however, use their ability to influence the employees that report to them, work beside them and who are above them in the corporate structure.

Leaders have the power to influence people in ways they may not understand. Great leaders influence their boss and their boss's boss, in ways that help the company reach greater levels of success. (See Figure 2)

Spheres of Influence

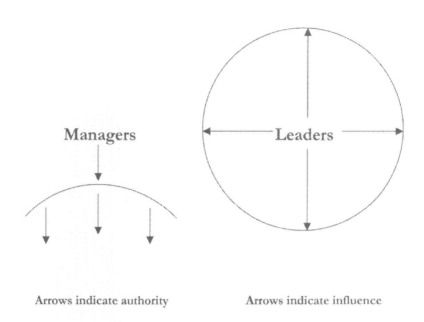

Arrows indicate authority   Arrows indicate influence

Figure 2

In addition to the influence you have at your company, a leader's greatest influence may come on a jobsite you actually never set foot on. The power of your leadership may have a positive influence on someone who achieves great things on another job in a different part of the country.

Alexander the Great, born in Macedonia in 356 B.C., was one of the most successful generals in history. He overthrew the Persian Empire and carried his campaign all the way to India. He assembled an empire larger than any other before him by the time he was thirty-two.

Yet Alexander was surely influenced and inspired by the generals, statesmen, and teachers that he learned from and that he learned about. For example, Alexander's father, Phillip II, was the influential king of Macedonia, and an important figure in the world at that time. Alexander's teacher from childhood to manhood was the philosopher Aristotle, who had in turn been a student of Plato.

Alexander would have learned from Aristotle about the Athenian general and statesman Pericles, born more than a hundred years earlier. Under the leadership of Pericles, the Athenian Empire reached the height of its cultural and imperial achievement.

Alexander would also have learned of the Persian king Darius III, born in 330 B.C., only twenty-six years before Alexander. The conquests of Darius extended Persian rule into modern Afghanistan and Pakistan, and it was Darius whom Alexander yearned to defeat—and did defeat—when he conquered Persia.

Given all this, the question then becomes, who actually had the most influence in determining the size of the empire of Alexander the Great? Was it Alexander himself, or was it his father's influence, through example and expectation, or was it the teacher he learned from, keeping in mind the fact that neither Phillip nor Aristotle had ever set foot in the far reaches of Alexander's ultimate empire?

Effective supervisors understand that their crew's

performance, good or bad, is a direct reflection on their ability to supervise. Failed job assignments, poor quality work or low morale means the supervisor has failed the company and its employees. If a department's performance is sub-par, the supervisor is responsible, and it is his job to turn performance around.

Effective supervisors understand what it is to be a leader, what it is to be a manager, and know how and when to be both.

The Supervisor's Role

The supervisor, whether she is a front-line supervisor, middle manager or department head, is responsible for managing the company's resources in a way that insures company profitability. The supervisor's role is to use management and leadership skills to provide the tools, materials, equipment and expectations of lofty achievement from the people who work for them.

"To the company you are 'their man' on the job. You are management, responsible for the success or failure of the company. . . . a decision-maker who can gain or lose profits, build or destroy company prestige, get ahead or fall behind on production and deal successfully with employees or cause turmoil.

To the people who work for you, the supervisor is 'the company.' They look to you for guidance and leadership on the job . . . . it's the supervisor's job to represent the company skillfully, honestly and fairly in order to get the best from your workers and thereby profit the company." [4]

The Supervisor and Expectations

Often new supervisors, and some experienced supervisors, don't understand that the job is about having expectations of achievement for the people that work for them. Many times they don't think ahead and care only about completing this week's tasks. Yet, if supervisors do not have high expectations of their employees, and communicate those expectations with a clear set of goals, they are setting up their company, their employees and themselves for failure.

To provide expectations for your employees, you must be aware of the business goals of the company, and the expectations placed on you by your own supervisors. The goals you set must focus employee energy in the same direction. Here are the expectations of the supervisor by the company and its employees: [5]

The company expects the supervisor to:

Plan the day's work in advance. Things that happen throughout the day should not be a constant surprise.

Manage resources properly. The proper management of labor, material, tools and equipment will reduce costs in every segment of the operation.

Maintain quality standards. Constant attention must be given to maintain the high-quality standards dictated by the company. Mistakes and re-work reduces the company's profitability and shortens the length of everyone's employment.

Improve methods of work. A supervisor has to be constantly on the watch for better ways of doing things in their efforts to keep costs down, quality up and production on schedule.

Get and keep the confidence and respect of their employees. A supervisor must not only have the aptitude to lead people, but must also have the ability to do it consistently, on a day-in-and-day-out basis.

Be a good communicator. A supervisor must have lofty yet achievable expectations and be able to communicate them with a clear set of goals. In addition to talking to their employees, supervisors must understand that a big part of communicating includes listening to the ideas and concerns of the employee.

Develop the skills of employees. A supervisor must not only utilize the talents of employees but must also help employees develop additional skills, in order to help build a continual stream of new supervisors. These future leaders are critical to a company's long-term success.

Employees expect their supervisor to:

Know his job. Employees respect a person who knows his job and does it well. They like to work for him because they can learn from him, as well as look up to him.

Treat employees with fair play. One of the quickest ways to lose respect for authority lies in seeing it used to coddle a favorite. Be prepared to do for all what you've done for one.

Give employees courteous and consistent treatment. Simple courtesy is a great time saver because it eliminates opposition before it starts. How about you? Would you rather be asked in a reasonable tone of voice or ordered about like a lackey?

Let employees know where they stand. No one likes to be kept in the dark about his actions. Simply letting an employee know whether he is doing a good job or a poor one can be the key to building morale or correcting a bad situation before it gets worse. Whether the news about him is good or bad, an employee deserves to know in order to be able to prepare for the future with confidence.

Discuss things openly and honestly. When an employee has a problem that he can't bring up with his supervisor because of fear or mistrust, the supervisor and the company has a problem. Always be sure to have time for a person to tell you what's on his mind and always allow him to speak freely without feeling that he may offend you.

Understand an individual's problems. Everybody has problems. The most important thing to remember is that when an employee has a problem, it is, in part, your problem too, because that problem may affect the way the job is performed. Showing an employee you understand his special needs goes a long way toward eliminating frustration and helps builds loyalty.

Appreciate and respect the contributions of each person to the job. If you show each employee that what they've done is important, whatever their job, you'll have much happier employees who will be willing to "walk that extra mile" to live up to your expectations and achieve the goals of the company.

Give recognition for a job well done. When an employee gets praise for doing good work, they'll continue to do good work. When they stop getting recognition for it, the quality of the work may decline.

Use discipline wisely. This is little more than being fair with your employees. Discipline should be thought of as a teaching method. Do all discipline in private. Berating a person in the presence of his fellow workers is a sure way to lose his willing cooperation forever. [6]

The Supervisor and Contradictions

Supervision is fraught with a jumbled maze of contradictions that often make it difficult to determine the best course for any given situation. You may think you are doing what is right, only to find out that there may have been other factors in play that should have been considered. It is not until you comprehend this swirling mass of contradictions that you will have the best chance of making the right decisions. I have already mentioned the two major roles of a supervisor, leading and managing. They are also two of the major contradictions of supervision, and inherent in them is the difficulty of deciding when to manage people and when to lead them. Here are several other contradictions that are important to understand while working in your role as supervisor.

Standardization versus Creativity

In any company the product or service provided must meet certain specifications that insure performance and profitability. In meeting these specifications, certain standards must be maintained. It is difficult for experienced workers, especially craftsmen, to be bound by written standards. They will tell you they have been doing the job for years and don't need anyone to tell them how to do it. Yet, invariably, quality specifications, when passed from one management generation to the next, without proper documentation, will fall below the minimum standards required.

Just as the manager works to control and measure employees, written standards should be in place to insure quality.

Creativity brings forth new and unexplored ideas. Creativity can improve service and product quality, yet creativity without minimum standards can leave performance short.

Each has its place, yet an absolute of either will fail to promote growth or prevent failure. It is up to you as supervisor to determine the appropriate mix of each.

Rules and Systems versus Flexibility

In the same way that standards are necessary to insure product quality, structured rules and systems are necessary to insure consistency and an understanding of policies. By the same token, however, structured systems, no matter how tried and tested, can never provide an answer for every situation. In certain situations, the only thing that will suffice is the flexibility to make the appropriate choice, at the appropriate time, for the given circumstance.

Centralization versus De-centralization

Throughout my career, the one thing that constantly challenged management was how to organize support departments. Should they be organized in a centralized structure or a de-centralized one?

Centralized departments are organized with one autonomous, central management team, which services multiple departments, or areas, and has its own management structure.

De-centralized departments, usually production departments, have their own support groups, each with managers that report to the department head.

It is important to understand that there is no best way to organize your support groups. You must select a structure that provides the advantages that best suit your needs, and then work to minimize its disadvantages.

The following are a few of the advantages and disadvantages of each type.

Centralized Support Organizations

Advantages

- Fewer employees can service more groups and areas
- Labor costs are reduced due to the ability to stretch labor resources
- Standards can be maintained due to tracking and enforcement by one management group
- Better able to look at big-picture priorities because they are not tied to just one group or area

Disadvantages

- Less able to provide top service because of limited resources stretched over several areas
- Employee ownership can suffer due to inability to focus in just one area
- The top priorities of one group may be overshadowed by the overall priorities of the company

De-centralized Support Organizations

Advantages

- Better service can be provided

- More employee ownership because of familiarity with one area's people and equipment

Disadvantages

- More costly
- Different areas maintain different standards of work depending on each area's management team

Companies that continually switch back and forth, constantly chasing the benefits of one structure or the other, are the biggest losers.

Command and Control versus Empowerment

Command and control versus empowerment is similar to managing versus leading. In managing, it is assumed that command and control will insure compliance with rules and hierarchal decision—making, and will maintain performance at optimum levels. Empowerment, like leading, opens up the playing field and turns much of the control over to employees in an effort to encourage better performance.

Effective supervisors assess each situation carefully to determine when control of a situation is necessary and when empowerment will encourage the effort to achieve greater results.

Empowerment versus Abandonment

Although empowerment can give your employees a feeling of control, and can motivate them to try harder, there is a point at which the absence of active interest by management may feel like abandonment. When employees have no feedback they become frustrated and unsure of whether they are making the right decisions.

Teamwork versus Accountability

Teamwork, overseen by management, is an essential element in achieving success. Without it, employees strive for their own personal success without thought of the success of their co-workers or the success of their company.

While teamwork is essential, care must be taken not to let teamwork become the only goal. When teamwork is more important than overall company performance, team members can begin to overlook failures in achieving the goals necessary for overall company success. They do this out of loyalty to their team members. They don't want to get fellow team members in trouble. In this situation, teamwork can foster the kind of patience that endures waste, and waste costs the company money. Each person must balance their responsibility to their team members with their responsibility to the company to ensure accountability.

Loyalty to People versus Responsibility to the Company

All supervisors hope to gain the loyalty of their employees, and all should strive to return it. However, loyalty to your group, at its extreme, may interfere with your responsibility to the company. Supervisors must keep in mind that their first responsibility is as profit managers for the company.

If supervisors begin placing their loyalty to their employees above their responsibility to the company, both will suffer. On the other hand, if they never show any loyalty, they will never receive any loyalty. If they show loyalty above all else, they can never be effective.

Core Duties versus Special Projects

One of the pitfalls of supervision is trying to be "all things to all people." Most supervisors are dedicated, hardworking employees, and they want to live up to their boss's expectations whenever possible. As responsible supervisors, however, you must take care not to forget your core duties: employee safety, employee conduct and employee performance on the job.

Sometimes management will ask more of its supervisors, in an effort to get additional projects completed. Supervisors may be tempted to postpone certain core duties in order to get special projects completed. Unfortunately, in most cases, what gets put on hold are the very duties you were hired to perform— duties such as being out on the floor or in the field, interacting with employees and ensuring safety and performance.

Your boss won't understand your situation or the choices you face, however, unless you let him know what is going on. If you don't tell your boss that you are overloaded, he will assume you are fulfilling your core responsibilities.

On the flip side, special projects can be the spawning ground for exciting work and future promotions. Special projects give the supervisor the opportunity to try new and interesting things and to use otherwise untapped skills and abilities. Special projects may showcase your organizational skills, or your ability to motivate and inspire other employees to bring a project in on time, or they may give you the opportunity to show how you can lead a team of employees to success.

To insure your personal success, and the success of your company, it is critical that you understand and perform your core duties. When you are stretched to the point that duties such as ensuring employee safety, employee conduct and employee performance must be neglected, talk to your supervisor and explain your situation.

At the same time, if given a special project, you should endeavor to work as hard as possible to make the project successful. This is important because special projects typically get more attention from middle and upper management, and it is important to leave a good impression, which will inevitably boost confidence in your abilities.

Failure to understand these contradictions of supervision will limit your ability to succeed. Learn from various situations, including the observation of how other supervisors handle these contradictions, and then consider the results of the various choices and actions. Size up each situation on a case-by-case basis, and then prepare yourself to make better decisions.

Chapter 2

The Cost of Ineffective Supervision

Just as effective supervision will improve employee efficiencies and company performance, ineffective supervision will cost more than if employees are left on their own. Ineffective supervision allows for, and often promotes, inefficiencies in the workplace. This adds up to employee frustration and diminished overall performance. Effective supervision is the company's best means to insure higher profits and reduced costs. Every minute an employee or a machine is unproductive it costs the company money. This seems simple to understand, yet not every supervisor realizes the serious impact that unproductive employees have on profitability and competitiveness.

Working Hard Isn't Enough

Most supervisors work hectic schedules every day. They run from job to job, crisis to crisis, rarely getting a spare moment to themselves. Overall, the supervisor's work ethic as a group is generally as high as any group of employees in the company. Even though most supervisors are hardworking and dedicated employees, that alone does not insure that they are effective in their role as supervisors.

Because supervisors interact with so many employees in the company, they have the greatest ability to influence job performance, positively or negatively, and therefore, overall company performance.

Because they work so hard, a supervisor can get defensive when asked how they can improve performance. For a supervisor to improve, it is important for her to understand that it doesn't matter how hard she works if that hard work doesn't result in the optimum performance and hard work of each of the employees that report to her.

Five Types of Company Loss

There are many types of loss that detract from company profitability. When manufacturing a product, or providing a service, the only thing that adds value is productive employee time that moves the process from one step to the next. The following losses detract from profitability: planned employee losses, unplanned employee losses, management system losses, quality losses, and regulatory, safety and environmental losses.

If supervisors fail to monitor and minimize company losses they are costing the company money and reducing the company's chance for success. Robert Wilson of Performance Consulting Associates points out that "Use of maintenance craft resources is . . . alarming: average craft productivity, measured through 'wrench time' studies, is typically in the 25 to 35 percent range. Productive work is held up by time spent waiting for materials, tools, instructions, and clearance and time traveling to the job."[7] That means for an average $32,000 salary, companies are benefiting from only $8,000 in productive employee labor.

Productive Employee Time

Productive employee time includes all time employees are actually working productively by operating, manufacturing, installing, servicing, maintaining, repairing or providing services. Productive employee time does not include parts searches, travel time or meetings.

Five Types of Company Loss

Planned Employee Losses—Planned employee losses are a part of the cost of doing business and include shift lineout, breaks, daily meetings, travel to and from jobs, paperwork and cleanup. It is the supervisor's job to manage effectively, and to minimize employee time losses.

Unplanned Employee Losses—This includes visiting and extended personal time after breaks, lunches and meetings. Excessive unplanned employee losses can be attributed directly to ineffective supervision.

Management System Losses—Management system losses include poor planning programs, poor employee selection processes, inadequate training programs and ineffective absenteeism programs.

Quality Losses—This includes losses from re-work due to a lack of quality standards, employee training, or employee inattentiveness. These losses represent hidden costs and can be attributed to both limited employee skills and inadequate management systems.

Regulatory, Safety and Environmental Loss—This includes the costs for regulatory compliance, medical costs for injuries, and the cost of environmental compliance and awareness. These costs are often hidden in production costs and are not easily quantified. The supervisor should always strive to minimize these costs by setting the highest standards of compliance.

Supervisor Effectiveness Rating

All of the previous losses, coupled with productive employee time, add up to the total time an employee is paid to produce a product or provide a service. On the Supervisor Effectiveness Rating Graph shown, you can see the difference between exceptional and ineffective management performance.

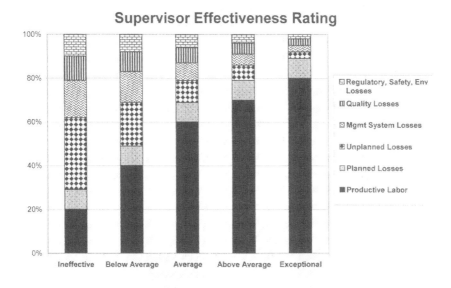

Figure 3[8]

To improve productivity, first assess your skills as a supervisor, then the quality of your management systems, and then determine where improvements should be made.

Once deficiencies are identified, an action plan for improvement can be built.

Supervisors who fail to correct performance problems are not doing their job, and that ends up costing their employers millions of dollars each year.

Chapter 3

Leadership Skills

Understanding People—The Supervisor

The performance of your employees is dependent upon your ability to motivate them. Each employee is different and requires different motivational techniques to achieve maximum productivity. Before you can understand how to motivate and inspire your employees, you first need to understand what kind of supervisor you are, and then make the necessary adjustments to become more effective. Here are the characteristics of three supervisor types:[9]

The "Tough Guy" Supervisor

1. Lacks tact
2. Lacks understanding
3. Jumps to conclusions
4. Disciplines employees in front of others
5. Creates dissension and resentment
6. Angry
7. Determined to succeed

Generally, the determination of this type of supervisor

is not worth the trouble they cause. A supervisor who is resentful, too abrupt, doesn't care to understand employees or doesn't use tact upsets the workforce emotionally. Workers become bewildered and confused to the point of rebellion. They ask themselves: "If he doesn't care about me, why should I care about him?" That begins a worrisome cycle that deteriorates the overall performance of the workforce.

The "Good Guy" Supervisor

1. Is too trusting
2. Lacks confidence
3. Is not observant
4. Too often depends on persuasion
5. Strives for conflict avoidance instead of working at conflict management
6. Doesn't correct poor performance or slacking off immediately

The "Good Guy" supervisor is usually too close to their employees personally to give them proper leadership. This supervisor would rather be a good buddy than the person in charge. They don't understand that they can't "ride the fence" and be a good supervisor at the same time. The end result is that their employees have more control than they do. The "Good Guy" supervisor may finally realize that he is being taken advantage of, but by then there is not much he can do about it.

The Effective Supervisor

The "Effective Supervisor" can strike the delicate balance

between the "Tough Guy" and the "Good Guy" supervisor types. They are as friendly and courteous as possible, but they are also respected for their position and how they carry themselves. They treat their employees fairly and consistently, but are known to be in charge and firm on seeing that orders are carried out quickly and efficiently. Their actions, words and prompt handling of situations make employees want to do what they ask of them.

Understanding People—The Employee

Having read the characteristics of the effective supervisor, and resolving to make plans to improve your approach with your employees, your next step should be to develop the skill to read and understand your employees. Each employee has different personality traits and skill levels. There are those who are skilled and effective at what they do and there are those who are still learning. There are those who are willing participants with good attitudes toward company goals, and there are those who couldn't care less what anyone wants of them. One of the keys to becoming a better supervisor is recognizing each type of employee and learning how to coach each for success. Here are the character traits of four different types of employees: [10]

The Uncooperative, Unskilled Employee

1. Belligerent
2. Sullen
3. Argumentative
4. Tactless

5. Low skill level
6. Sloppy workmanship
7. Inefficient
8. Unsafe

This type of employee has the highest chance for failure, not only because of his lack of skills, but also because of the problems he causes with the rest of the crew. The supervisor's goal with this individual should be to set recognizable goals, related to both attitude and skill level, discuss them openly with the employee and develop an action plan. If the employee demonstrates that he can't make the improvements necessary, you must make a quick decision. You can't keep this employee long because he is being paid for what he doesn't know, and his bad attitude is detrimental to the rest of the crew.

The Cooperative, Unskilled Employee

1. Responsive
2. Lighthearted
3. Congenial
4. Sympathetic
5. Low skill level
6. Sloppy workmanship
7. Inefficient
8. Unsafe

Supervisors, especially those with less experience, spend most of their time with this employee because they appreciate support from their employees as much as they appreciate skill. Because of that support they sometimes allow this employee to "get by." If this happens, the rest of the crew will soon recognize that you are not holding this employee to the same standard and will begin to resent your lack of leadership. You must set recognizable skill level improvements. If the employee shows improvement, praise his effort and set higher goals. If he doesn't improve, you have a decision to make.

The Uncooperative, Skilled Employee

1. Belligerent
2. Sullen
3. Argumentative
4. Tactless
5. High skill level
6. Good workmanship
7. Effective
8. Safe

This is generally the most difficult employee to deal with. They are the "Tough Guys" on the crew. Their skill level demands that you show respect for their knowledge, but their attitude can demoralize the whole crew. Allowing the perception that this person is in control will undermine, and limit, your ability to be effective with the rest of the crew. Quick action is essential. Be firm, but allow an opening for friendliness. Don't hesitate to put them in their place, but do it in private. Play up their good qualities and don't return their example of un-cooperativeness. Talk to them about their effect on people and give them goals to reach. If they are worth saving, you should see rapid improvement.

The Cooperative, Skilled Employee

1. Responsive
2. Lighthearted
3. Congenial
4. Sympathetic
5. High skill level
6. Good workmanship
7. Efficient
8. Safety conscious
9. Effective leader

This is the employee you ask the most of because he consistently delivers. He understands what you want and does it that way. This person is generally the unofficial leader of the group and the next person in line for promotion. Use his attitude and work ethic as an example to the others on the crew. Because he is so helpful, you may feel compelled to do extra for this employee, but putting this employee above the rules places both of you in an uncomfortable position. Be prepared to do for all what you have done for one.

It is imperative that supervisors understand how critical it is for them to make a commitment to improve their own skills, and the skills and performance of the employees in their group. Failure means that you are letting your employees down, you are letting your employer down, and, above all, you are letting yourself down.

Motivational Communication Skills

In order to become a skilled leader, you must learn and

master motivational communication. Tone of voice, presence, self-confidence, and gestures are standard "tools of the trade." This craft, properly used, can inspire employees to reach their highest potential. Failing to acquire this skill means you will probably fall short of your potential success, which will work to limit the success of your company.

Good leaders appear natural, at ease and self-confident in their delivery, and while speaking skills may come naturally to some, others will need to work at them. If stirring oratory can inspire men and women to give the ultimate sacrifice for someone or something they believe in, it can surely help motivate your workforce to greater performance. Some assert that these skills are critical to being effective. In "How Lincoln Won the War with Metaphor," James M. McPherson quotes Southern historian David M. Potter, "If the Union and Confederacy had exchanged presidents with one another, the Confederacy might have won its independence."[11] McPherson continues, "Most historians would probably agree with Potter's general point that Jefferson Davis's shortcomings as a leader played a role in the Confederate defeat. They would agree that one of Davis's principle failures was an inability to communicate effectively with other Confederate leaders and with the Southern people."[12] McPherson goes on, "It is no coincidence that Lincoln and Roosevelt were great war presidents who led the United States to its most decisive victories in its most important wars. Their preeminent quality as leaders was an ability to communicate the meanings and purposes of these wars in an intelligible, inspiring manner that helped energize and mobilize their people to make the sacrifices necessary for victory."[13] . . .

By contrast, Jefferson Davis failed to do a good job in 'eliciting the enthusiasm and energies of the people'."[14]

Is there any reason to believe that being effective in these skills will not work to motivate your workforce to greater performance?

The following are four examples of oratory that show how words, spoken with skill, have moved people. The sincerity of the speakers and the eloquence of their words stress the importance of remaining calm, in the first case, and the importance of taking action, in the latter. [15]

- Franklin D. Roosevelt's first inaugural address on March 4, 1933, refers to the deepening depression that began after the disastrous financial crash of 1929, an event that left millions devastated and the country on the brink of ruin. With his elegant, aristocratic and self-confident voice, Roosevelt calmed a fearful nation when he assured them, "The only thing we have to fear is fear itself."

- In an inspirational speech on August 28, 1968, Doctor Martin Luther King used his deep, thundering voice to speak to the wave of humanity gathered during the Civil Rights Peace March on the mall in Washington, D.C.: "When we let freedom ring," he told them, "when we let it ring from every village and every hamlet, from every state and every city, we will be able to speed up that day when all of God's children, black men and white men, Jews and Gentiles, Protestants and Catholics, will be able to join hands and sing the words of that old Negro spiritual, Free at last! Free at last! Thank God Almighty, we are free at last!"

- John F. Kennedy's Democratic nomination acceptance

speech on July 15, 1960, delivered in his charming New England accent, inspired and encouraged his party members, and the nation, and let them know, "The New Frontier of which I speak is not a set of promises—it is a set of challenges. It sums up not what I intend to offer to the American people, but intend to ask of them." He followed up this theme as president in January of 1961, speaking one of the most famous inaugural lines ever in his address to the nation, "And so, my fellow Americans, ask not what your country can do for you, ask what you can do for your country."

Roosevelt inspired a nation and helped them get through the Great Depression and World War II, King inspired Blacks and Whites to come together in an effort to expand Civil Rights, and Kennedy inspired a generation to reach for the stars—and the moon—and to give up their own comfort by helping others while serving in the Peace Corps.

Similarly, in business, Lee Iacocca used leadership skills to turn a reeling Chrysler Corporation around in the late '70s and early '80s. Jack Welch inspired GE employees in the early eighties to reach up out of mediocrity to become one of the premier examples of the successful company in the '80s and '90s. Gordon Bethune used his leadership skills to pull Continental Airlines out of a nosedive which had them headed for their third bankruptcy in a decade, and righted the airline so it could score record-breaking profits.

Can you visualize yourself communicating in a similar manner in an effort to motivate those who look to you for their inspiration? Here are some tips that will help you prepare yourself for motivational speaking.

TIPS ON PREPARING AND DELIVERING A SPEECH

"Pick a topic you know well and feel strongly about— It is easier to talk about something you know well and feel strongly about than to try to fool the audience. If you don't know what you're talking about you really have no business wasting the audience's time. If you don't feel strongly about your topic you can't expect your audience to feel anything either. If you have to speak about something you know little about, do some research and if you can't master your topic, admit it and stick to the aspects you do know.

Summon up some emotion—If you feel strongly about something let it show. Get angry, happy, and emotional. Gesture. Raise your voice. A speech is not just words. Gestures and vocal variety make your speech interesting.

Use personal examples—You know these well and you can remember your feelings.

Use stories—Stories stay with us longer than simple facts.

Use props—Pictures, objects, anything that can help illustrate what you are talking about. Give a demonstration, act something out, ask us to imagine an object if you can't show us.

Know your audience—Speak to them individually ahead of time. Discuss what you will be talking about and ask for feedback and ideas. Use language and examples your audience will understand.

Prepare and use notes—List your main points on index cards or paper or use flip charts or slides.

Open with an attention grabber—Give some thought to the first thing you will say. You might use a joke, but choose one that relates to your topic. The attention grabber does not have to be flashy, just something that you know the audience can relate to.

State your main point and repeat, repeat, repeat—You should be able to state the objective of your speech in a single simple sentence. You elaborate in the body of the speech and end with the simply stated objective.

Compose yourself—Take a deep breath, look around. You can take a moment before you begin and you can pause when you need to.

After it is over get feedback—Learn what people liked and remembered. It will surprise you. Ask for suggestions and ways you could improve." [16]

TIPS ON MOTIVATING A GROUP WITH A SPEECH

"Answer the audience's question 'What's in it for me?'[17]—Appeal to the self-interest of your listeners.

Appeal to their pride—Tell them you need their skills.

Maintain a positive attitude—Acknowledge how they may feel about a difficult job but don't let them control the attitude. Good morale is when you think you can do something.

Explain in sufficient detail what you want and offer support—It's your job to ensure that they have the resources to do what you ask of them and that you are clear and direct in your request.

Make it personal—Look them in the eyes, use their names, ask directly for their help. This is not the same as asking to do work as a personal favor but it should be known that they work for you and not a faceless company and that they are accountable to you and the others on the crew." [18]

The Prime Motivators

During Pickets Charge at the Battle of Gettysburg, thousands of Southerners charged across a mile of rolling hills towards a stonewall and possible death. What was it that motivated these men to risk and often give their lives? Was it money? Was it fame? We know it was not. Front-line Civil War soldiers didn't get rich and most did not gain fame. So what drove them to charge into battle?

I believe their primary motivation was the expectations of their leaders, their peers, and their families. They were also strongly motivated by their own expectations of themselves. They took pride in accomplishing something that was important to them. They were expected to be brave and loyal. Most were. Throughout history, millions of men and women have made the ultimate sacrifice because of the expectations of authority and their own sense of duty and pride.

Does the same thing apply in a work environment? Will most men and women work hard because you are their leader and they don't want to let you down? In most cases they will. While many people find it difficult to feel loyalty towards a company, most can feel loyalty towards a person they trust. Effective leaders tap into that. Most employees have a basic desire to please those in authority and do so by trying to live up to your expectations. Some will not and so a different strategy is required for them. However, generally, if it's a priority for the supervisor, it's a priority for the employee.

If being the best is your primary goal that will be the primary goal of your employees. If you appeal to their sense of pride and promote your desire to be the hardest-working, best-performing group in the company, most of your employees will do everything in their power to help you achieve that goal. On the other hand, if they see you fighting with your fellow supervisors, or being lazy, or playing silly games, they will take those to be your priorities and will make those their main priorities as well.

What about money? Is money a prime motivator? Is money the magical remedy for all the de-motivated employees in your company? Rarely. Money is important for getting employees to come to your company or for countering turnover in a strong job market where other companies are providing aggressive pay packages, but it doesn't help motivate your work force to be more productive or inspire them to positive attitudes. If money were the answer, top earners would always work harder and have better attitudes than lower-paid workers. That isn't the case and in many instances quite the opposite is true. Some highly paid employees believe that they are "owed" the top wage they receive, and they shouldn't have to do anything to get it.

You should look toward things like employee pride and your own expectations to motivate your employees. For employees to be proud, you have to set them up in an environment where they are able to excel in their work. If people are in a system where they can't excel, then they can't be proud of their accomplishments. People who work in systems that allow them to excel, and then are expected to excel, will be motivated to reach the highest success levels possible and will be proud when they do.

Pride and your expectations are the prime motivators that drive people toward achieving goals, whether it is achieving record-breaking production targets or storming a hill on a battlefield.

I can remember the owner of the first electrical contractor I ever worked for. He was a short, large, red-haired man with a wonderful personality. He was always enthusiastic and excited about the job, his company and its employees. One morning when I was still in the first year of my apprenticeship, he came to the job, walked up, put his big bear-like arm around me and said to my journeyman and me "You guys are doing a super job. Come on, I'm going to take you to breakfast." The impact of that gesture, and other gestures he made throughout the time I knew him, has stayed with me for 25 years and to this day I can still remember feeling proud as I visualize his arm enveloping my shoulders, and I still remember looking down at his big right hand and his big stubby fingers, with red freckles, lying across my chest. Because he understood people and how to motivate them, I wanted to make him proud of me and I believe I would have done almost anything for him.

If motivation is a problem with your employees, look at the expectations you have of them and the attitude you have toward their achievement and success. Clarify your expectations, set your employees up in a system in which they can excel, and make sure they can take pride in their accomplishments.

The Pitfalls of Implied Consent

Too often supervisors fail to understand that one of their greatest influences with employees lies in the actions they don't take. Every time a supervisor tolerates inappropriate behaviors they imply to that person, and everyone else who sees it, that this type of behavior is acceptable. For example, if you walk past an employee who is not using the proper safety equipment and say nothing, you are, by your lack of action, giving your implied consent for the actions they took. To be successful, you must communicate your expectations to your employees and call them on behavior that doesn't live up to those expectations.

Have you ever given implied consent for inappropriate behavior? Have you ever stood by while employees were standing around when they should have been working? Have you ever witnessed, and even joined in, when others were belittling the company or their fellow employees? Not only does this type of behavior contribute to the degeneration of morale, it also limits the company's ability to succeed. If supervisors, who are the company's representatives, allow employees to loaf, stand around visiting or belittling their employer, they will diminish their authority and soon lose the confidence of their employees in their ability to lead. This lack of leadership breeds contempt toward the company. That contempt erodes the employee's faith in the company's ability to succeed, and of its supervisors to make the right business decisions. Instead, a supervisor must always:

- Make it clear that you won't tolerate unproductive, unsafe or negative behavior.

- Make it clear that employees and co-workers conduct themselves in a professional and business-like manner.
- Enforce your expectations by setting examples and taking action.

Be Firm but Fair

Of all management philosophies, let this one guide you in your actions when dealing with employees. Let your employees know that you are a reasonable person, somewhat forgiving of their weaknesses, but at the same time resolved in your expectations that they perform their duties to the highest possible level of effectiveness. Remember, part of your job is to make it a good place for all employees to work. One important way to do that is to praise work that is well done, and reprove unproductive or destructive attitudes and behavior.

Emotions as Tools

One of the motivating factors for most employees is their desire to please those in authority. They want to do a good job for you and have you recognize them for it. You can tap into that employee pride by understanding that your emotions, used in a positive way, are tools you can use to motivate employees. These tools include enthusiasm, excitement, determination, frustration, happiness, disappointment and anger.

To be able to use these tools you must first step back and take an objective look at your own reactions in different situations. Do you flare up at the least provocation or does everything roll off your back? If you always appear overly calm and unmoved regardless of the situation, your employees will interpret this as a lack of interest. If you show enthusiasm when enthusiasm is appropriate, anger when anger is appropriate, your workers will respond to your leadership.

Next, you must analyze how your reactions in various situations affect the attitude and productivity of your employees. Your emotions should work for you, not against you. Instead, use emotions in a positive way. In order to become the most effective supervisor you can be, learn to control your emotions instead of letting them control you.

While it impossible to neatly sort all supervisors into narrow, one-size-fits-all slots, we can for the purpose of our discussion here, see them falling into a few wide and general categories. Of the many supervisors I have observed over the years, the most frustrated and ineffective is the angry reactionary. In fact, I've seen crews deliberately "work" these supervisors on purpose just to see them go off the deep end. It almost becomes a sport for some employees.

Make sure you can recognize when people are trying to "work" you. Be careful not to get mad every time something goes wrong. Once employees know how easily you lose control it becomes a joke to them. When that happens you lose credibility and your ability to lead is undermined.

Adjust your style by watching and learning how other supervisors deal with situations, both positively and negatively. Hold back anger for those situations where you think anger is the appropriate tool. Use enthusiasm to charge your workforce up. Learn how, where and when to use different emotions to motivate your employees.

The Workplace Class System

One of the great things about living in America is our ideal of equality. We believe that everyone should be treated equally. Yet at work, as in other areas of our lives, the ideal is seldom achieved. You don't have to look far to see that top management is treated more favorably than the custodial staff.

Class systems exist in our workplaces today because of the different levels of responsibility in the company. As pay and authority levels rise, so does the level of responsibility. Skilled workers are essential in the workplace, but they are only responsible for the quality of their own work. Upper-level positions in a company are responsible for everyone's performance, as well as their safety, and the company's compliance with local, state and federal regulations. It is important for companies to compete for talent, and pay and authority are important parts of that system of competition.

By the same token, however, most American workers find class systems distasteful, especially when they perceive an "I'm better than you" attitude. Most employees in the lower tiers of a company structure can live with a class system, as long as they don't have it constantly thrown in their face. Pride is a prime motivator, and if your actions are perceived as an attempt to put an employee down, you are promoting a culture of dissension.

Minimizing the Effects of the Workplace Class System

What can supervisors do to minimize the effects of the class system at their workplace? One of the greatest antidotes to a negative workplace class system is as simple as just being friendly. Sometimes supervisors don't understand the impact their attitudes have on employees and their productivity. We have excuses for not being friendly to those around us. We make excuses for not saying hello to someone we pass in the hallway because we don't know them well enough, or the person seemed unfriendly, or we "space it" because we are just too busy. But this lack of common courtesy is usually perceived as arrogance. This perceived arrogance filters down, and soon you are that rude SOB that thinks he is better than everyone else. When employees have that perception of their management staff, it is very difficult to nurture loyalty and a team culture.

To minimize this perception, everyone in a position of authority, from the CEO to front-line supervisors, must exercise great effort, encounter after encounter, to treat all employees in a friendly manner that exemplifies respect. This effort multiplies its impact, as others who witness it are encouraged. This translates into better employee relations, an atmosphere of loyalty and higher productivity.

The Do'ers versus the Be'ers

When it comes to doing work, there are two types of people in the world, the *Do'ers* and the *Be'ers*. The largest percentage of people are *Do'ers*—those people who are self-motivated, enjoy the work they do and work hard everyday. They are the people who like to get "down and dirty"; they are the people who get the job done. The rest are *Be'ers*—those people who are more interested in acting important and talking about themselves, than working hard.

To insure you gain, and keep, the respect of your co-workers, re-assess your attitude and work ethic. If you want to be an effective supervisor, make sure you are considered by everyone to be a *Do'er*.

Double Standards

In your effort to make the right choices, remember, if it's not right for your employees, it's not right for you, no matter how much power you have. Many front-line, middle and senior management supervisors believe that because they have a higher position in the company, they don't have to follow the same rules as everyone else. Quite the opposite is true. Each supervisor owes it to the company, and their employees, to set the highest example of compliance. People respond as much to what they see you do, as to what you tell them to do.

Employees get discouraged and angry when supervisors fail to follow the same rules they preach about. Nothing promotes class separation and dissension more quickly than a double standard. Rank deserves no privileges when it comes to policies and procedures.

Minimize the negative effects of the workplace class system by eliminating it wherever possible. You can do this by:

- Being friendly to everyone, everyday.
- Saying hello to everyone you pass, whether you know him or not. Remember, even if you don't know him, he probably knows you.
- Learning as many names as you can.
- Never letting your haste prevent you from being

courteous. That kind of thoughtless behavior is interpreted as arrogance.

- Taking an interest in the things that most interest your employees: their families, their hobbies, etc.
- Making it a point to be a *Do'er* not a *Be'er.*
- Understanding that if it's a rule for the employees, it's a rule for you, no exceptions.

The Myth of Morale

Is the morale of your workforce low? If so, what is your definition of morale and how do you measure it?

These are the questions that need to be asked before you tackle the issue of morale. Too often supervisors are confused about what morale is. "Some supervisors mistakenly believe that morale equals comfort"[19] and therein lies the myth of morale.

Thorndike Barnhart's definition of morale is: "moral or mental condition in regard to courage, confidence, enthusiasm, etc." [20] Nowhere in this definition, or in any other, will you find the word *comfort.*

Here is how we will define employee morale: **The energy, enthusiasm, loyalty, confidence and action generated by the belief that management has the ability to lead their employees, their department and their company to success.**

Defined that way, do you have low morale in your department? If you do, perhaps it's because you have not conveyed a sense of confidence that your management team can lead the employees, the department, and the company to success. When you understand that morale is a barometer of your employee's confidence in your leadership, you can no longer blame the General Manager or the corporate office for low morale. The morale of your employees is clearly your responsibility as their supervisor.

Morale Equals Success / Success Equals Efficiency

If a strong sense of enthusiasm, confidence and loyalty in accomplishing the tasks at hand is what's required to improve morale, what can you do to help promote confidence?

First, what is the common goal? Isn't the common goal of any company success? And isn't success defined by the achievement of company goals and objectives? If success is our common goal, what actions are necessary to achieve that goal? First, it is necessary that you and the rest of the management staff organize your resources so employees can be efficient in their work.

Second, it is necessary to assess the expectations of the majority of your workers. Do most of your employees hope that the company will be so disorganized and inefficient that it will take all day for them to get a small project done? Does the average employee sit around and think, "Gee, I hope my boss is so bad at his job that he can't find anything for me to work with so I can sit around and drink coffee all day long?"

Most employees aren't like that at all. They understand it is their supervisor's job to organize the work, which will help each of them be efficient and productive. When their management team is disorganized most workers get frustrated and can't understand why the company can't "get its act together." Most employees want to be efficient, and all employees understand that it's your job to keep them productive. If their company is the best at what it does, employees take pride in the fact they are a part of the company and its success.

Four Things Supervisors Should Understand About Morale

These basic tenets can help you nurture positive employee morale.

- Understand that employee morale is your responsibility as supervisor.
- Understand that low morale can result when employees feel their management team does not have the ability to lead them to success.
- Understand that you must create and maintain systems that foster the efficiency of your employees.
- Understand that employees must feel that their contributions are important and appreciated.

Finally, you must prove to your employees that, not only do you understand these requirements; you are capable of meeting them. Morale is built with enthusiasm, efficiency, and the recognition of the contributions of all to the single goal of success.

Attitude is a Choice

We all have problems in our lives, but some people seem to believe their own problems deserve more attention than the problems of everyone else. They also seem to believe that everyone at work is anxious to hear about them. While these people make a fuss over nothing, others handle their problems at work, as well as their problems at home, quietly and in private. Perhaps people who whine loudly simply like the attention, whether the attention is good or bad. Perhaps they want to feel that the world revolves around them? Whatever their motivation, it's a pity they don't understand that they are limiting their own chance for promotion, for interesting special projects, and most importantly, they are limiting their own chance for happiness and success.

While we cannot choose the attitude and behavior of others, we can choose our own. We can choose to love our work and all of its challenges. Always keep in mind that attitude is not only a choice, it is contagious, and spreads rapidly for good or ill. Your decision to keep your attitude positive will make you more marketable and put you ahead of your competition.

Chapter 4

Managerial Skills

Organizing Work Effectively

As a supervisor you have the responsibility to insure company profit through the combined use of company resources, employee time, materials, tools and equipment.

Poor organization, inefficient scheduling and wasted time all cost companies millions of dollars every year. While some dead time is unavoidable, it must be kept at a minimum. Necessary dead time, as described earlier, includes lineout time, breaks, cleanup, etc. Job stoppages due to lack of organization, or because of inefficient systems, waste time and resources that add unnecessary costs. Your employees can't perform beyond the boundaries of the system you've put them in, no matter how talented they are. (See Figure 1)

Each supervisor should evaluate how much time is being lost on his crew, or in his department, because of loose supervision and deficient organizational systems. Once that is determined, corrections can be made that allow your employees to reach their full potential. This is done by emphasizing work planning for every activity that occurs during your shift. From a previous section you will recall your role is to provide expectations for lofty achievement. You can't expect lofty achievement, if the systems your employees are working in are not providing tools and materials when they need them. Learn how to organize your resources and expect the same of others, and you will increase every employee's chance to complete each job successfully.

"Remember:
Plan your Work—then—Work your Plan" [21]

"When the Plan controls the Work, *the Work follows—in order.*
When the Work controls the Plan, *the Man follows—in chaos.*" [22]

Scheduling is more than just jotting down a few jobs and lining employees out in the morning. Planning involves more than just ordering a few parts and making a few phone calls. Supervising requires both, and involves sitting down prior to the start of each shift, exchanging information with those who will be impacted by your plans, and then carefully calculating how to use the available manpower, material and equipment, to determine how to achieve the goals for the day. In addition, it is important to understand that not all employees, materials or pieces of equipment will be available on any given shift. Successful supervisors build plans that provide for contingencies that will help them react to changing resources and unplanned events.

After the job is planned and ready to be implemented, each supervisor must set a minimum standard of performance for her employees. To help you determine the appropriate expectations you should have for your employees, ask yourself the following questions about company losses:

"Time losses:"

- Do your employees report on time?
- Do you question and straighten out absenteeism?
- Do you make sure your employees are properly equipped when they reach the job?
- Do you intentionally permit employees to do less work than they can?
- Do you limit visiting and conversation on the job to a reasonable minimum?
- Do you keep your employees waiting for job orders, equipment or materials?
- Do you give proper instructions in order to have your employees carry out the work?
- Do you permit unnecessary overtime?
- Do you make sure your employees are working efficiently until quitting time?
- Do you assign the right employees to the right jobs?
- Do you see that your employees are properly supplied with tools and equipment to do the job?
- Is your own time used effectively?

Material losses:

- Do your employees understand the value of materials they are working with?
- Do you permit careless and wasteful use of materials?
- Do you keep materials in a safe place?

- Do you check for defective material when it is delivered?
- Do you have a system to prevent loss or theft of materials?
- Do you permit waste or scrap to become excessive?
- Do you return excess materials to stock?
- Do you stage your crew's materials in an organized fashion?

Equipment and Tool losses:

- Do you instruct your employees on the proper care and handling of equipment and tools?
- Do you permit equipment to be abused?
- Do you inspect equipment periodically?
- Do you emphasize the value of equipment and tools?
- Do you use unserviceable tools and equipment?
- Do you schedule the use of equipment and tools so they are available on time?
- Do you make sure tools are accounted for and stored "properly at the end of the day?" [23]

Don't Just Schedule Work—Plan It

If you want to turn your department into a profit center you must first become better at planning the work that is generated. This can only be done by making it a priority for every level throughout the organization, not just the employee who has the title of "Planner." Every employee who supervises people, either directly or indirectly, should strive to become a more organized, more effective planner.

If not, the end result is a poorly executed project, installation or repair. Unplanned, unorganized jobs can cost up to twenty times more than effectively planned jobs. The benefit of effectively planned work is a reduced cost per task multiplied by the number of the times the job is performed each year. If done properly the net savings will be substantial. But to benefit, planners and supervisors must be effective. There is no benefit in hiring and paying supervisors to schedule and plan work if the end result is still unorganized jobs that requires parts, tools and material searches.

Scheduling

Scheduling is the assignment of employees, tools and equipment for a particular job on a given day. Just because you scheduled your work, however, it doesn't mean you have planned the work effectively. Scheduling helps reduce production and manufacturing losses but it does not assure the maximum amount of work in the least amount of time.

Planning

Planning is the effort made to pre-determine man-hours, tools, equipment, materials and job sequences for a given job, well in advance of the job's start time, through the use of any and all available information sources, including maintenance employees, operations employees, historical data, support services, vendors, etc. While planning helps make jobs more efficient, it won't be of much use if the work does not come off at the appropriately scheduled time to minimize production and manufacturing losses.

Effectively Organized Work

Effectively organized work is the result of intensive scheduling and planning efforts. It is that work which has been scheduled to minimize production losses and planned down to the last detail to provide efficient, low cost project implementation. This type of detailed planning and scheduling rolls all the best of the best into your job organization system and provides for the most cost effective use of your workforce.

Analyzing the Work—Before you can effectively plan for the work at hand you must first break the repair, installation or project down into separate phases. If you fail to identify all the phases of a job, you may miscalculate manpower, material or tool estimates. Only then can you order materials, determine manpower and equipment availability, and weave lead times into upcoming schedules.

Refining the Plan—The next phase is getting the feedback of those who will be expected to carry out the plan. While the plan is still formative, you should begin to communicate it to everyone who will be involved. This will help everyone understand why you have structured the plan the way you have, and resistance won't begin to grow.

Your employees have information vital to the plan that is only understood by someone who is around the work everyday. Prepare for meeting with your employees by putting together a list of questions. Getting input and buy-in will eliminate many of the surprises that may otherwise come up.

Implementing the Plan—If the work is properly organized, the work will be the easiest of all of the steps taken. That is not to say you won't have issues. No plan is foolproof. Effective scheduling and planning helps you organize your work and prepare for the unplanned events you are bound to encounter throughout the course of each job. If the plan does not include contingency planning, those responsible for implementing the plan cannot be successful.

Informational Communication Skills

In the previous section you learned that you must communicate the appropriate information to give each plan the best chance for success. Strong-willed supervisors take this to mean they should *talk* until everyone is completely worn out and give up trying to inject any input. Nothing could be further from the truth. To be a good informational communicator you must possess the ability to listen to others and understand what they are trying to tell you.

Listening is an art form and needs constant practice. You should endeavor to improve, much as you might practice your golf game.

Guidelines for Effective Listening

Silence is golden. You can't hear what someone is trying to say if you are talking. Learning to be silent, and trying to absorb and understand what the speaker is attempting to say—on the surface, and below the surface—will give you the advantage of additional valuable information. It is also a good way to build alliances, as speakers tend to appreciate someone who is willing to listen.

Drill down to find hidden information. Much of the

information you need will not be readily discernable on the surface. You should drill down to find hidden information by asking questions that lead the speaker to fill in the information gaps you have.

Learn to listen with your eyes. When people are speaking they use two distinct languages. They use spoken language and they use body language. When the speaker is having trouble communicating what they want to say, use your eyes to read their body language and strive to understand what they are trying to tell you.

Responding to the speaker visually. Just as you can pick up signals from the speaker visually, you can also send information visually that will promote better communication. Make eye contact with the speaker to let her know you are interested in what she is saying to you. Don't fidget, fuss or look around the room while people are speaking. Send the visual message that there is nothing more important than what the speaker is saying to you at that moment by giving her your undivided attention.

Meeting Skills

The ability to run a well-organized, fruitful meeting will benefit everyone who participates. Good meetings, where valuable information is exchanged, will help everyone be more successful at the tasks at hand. Here are some tips that will help you increase the value of your meetings.

The Manager's Role in a Meeting

Keep information flowing—In meetings, the manager must keep as much information flowing as possible by asking questions and inviting answers. Your job is to keep pressing until you get as much valuable information as it takes to put together a polished plan.

Let your co-workers know you want their opinion—If you simply invite your co-workers to a meeting and then drop your plan on them, without allowing for any discussion, you will end up with a poorly organized job.

Make a point of going through the current plan task by task to get feedback on things that can make the plan better.

Put those involved with your meetings at ease—Make sure they know your job is to listen, understand and respond to their needs. Even if what they ask is impossible, you must help them understand why it is impossible. Motivate those around you to care about whether the job is done right.

Expect your co-workers to show up at meetings—Everyone complains about having to go to meetings, but they also complain if you don't keep them in the loop. If your co-workers don't show up at a meeting, call them on the radio or phone and ask when they can arrive. If you leave everyone with the impression their input is important, and that you can't start the meeting without them, they will make sure to continue attending upcoming meetings and will work harder to provide valuable information.

Meeting time is restricted for information exchange and goal setting—Make sure the meeting is professional. Always start the meeting on time. Start by describing the upcoming work, and then ask questions that will help get the ball rolling. Make sure everyone participates. If those you have invited want to "visit" make sure they do it after the meeting.

Make it a goal to get and give as much information as possible—Getting as much, or more, information as you give is the true measure of the effectiveness of your meetings.

If you follow the guidelines listed, you will assure your co-workers that they have not wasted their time by attending your meetings and that you value the information they contribute. Value the time and opinion of your guests and you will gain their respect. The net result will be more organized work, and the building of important alliances that will insure everyone's success.

The Meeting Place

What your meeting place says to your guests can have a profound impact on your ability to achieve your meeting goals. A meeting place that is clean, bright and set up for guests will motivate your co-workers to actively participate in your planning sessions.

Attitude

The proper attitude toward your co-workers is very important for achieving success. It is not good enough to act as if your meeting guests are welcome, they must actually be welcome. Remember, attitude is a choice. No one looks forward to a meeting that may take important time from their other activities, where they feel unwelcome, and where their input is not appreciated.

"We" Instead of "Us and Them"

If an antagonistic relationship exists between departments,

each group may feel vindicated by the failure of the other. That group will profess, "I told you they were wrong!"

But what does that accomplish? The end result is a company product that is not as good as it could have been. One of the easiest lessons to overlook is that when one group loses, everyone loses. The failure of any department will eventually be shared by all, resulting in the loss of profitability and jobs.

Eliminating Hidden Waste

James P. Womack told the attendees at a Lean Conference in 1999, "To become lean we need only to think back to the early days of our business, chances are you were pretty lean back then." James Womack is an MIT professor who studied Toyota, its leaders and their method of building cars. In the books *The Machine that Changed the World* and *Lean Thinking* Womack and co-author Daniel T. Jones show their readers how the Japanese design their systems to stay efficient and operate with lower costs.

They point out that Toyota carmaker Taiichi Ohno identified seven types of waste:

- "**Defects** (in products)
- **Overproduction** of goods not needed
- **Inventories** of goods awaiting further processing or consumption
- **Unnecessary processing**
- **Unnecessary movement** (of people)
- **Unnecessary transport** (of goods)
- **Waiting** (by employees for process equipment to finish its work or on an upstream activity)" [24]

Lean thinkers Womack and Jones added an eighth type of waste:

- "The design of goods and services which do not meet user's needs." [25]

And, from my own experience, a ninth type of waste:

- Gathering information that is not used for anything.

Many times, we are so used to working in the systems we have developed, we have trouble seeing the inefficiencies that have been built in. We walk past waste everyday and never recognize that it is there or that it is costing the company money. "Lean Thinking" is the identification and elimination of waste in every form. But if we are too used to looking at waste, we won't really see it, and we won't be moved to eliminate it. "Lean Thinking" gives us a different view of our workplace by helping us identify the things that add cost, but no value, to our products.

Batch and Queue versus Continuous Flow [26]

In *"Lean Thinking"* Womack and Jones show how batch processing allows the build-up of inventory and promotes re-handling. In batch processing you see all of the seven wastes described by Ohno. "Lean Thinkers" recommend that all production systems eliminate any form of batch processing and move toward a system of continuous flow. This will help to eliminate the inherent costs of the seven types of waste.

An example of batch processing versus continuous flow

can be seen in modern McDonald's drive-thru windows. The traditional drive-thru window has one person with a headset that places the order, gathers the food and serves the customers. They batch process your order. In some newer McDonald's, however, there are three windows, one for ordering, one for paying and one for pickup. This is an example of continuous flow. Tests show that while having three employees in the three-window setup can be a bit more costly because of the additional labor dollars, it shaves time off customer delivery, allowing more customers to be served faster to improve customer service and increase revenue. Using all three windows during busy drive-thru periods of the day focuses on the needs of the customer and helps McDonalds stay more competitive.

Continuous Improvement Efforts

Employee Resistance

Employers have been working to involve the workforce in continuous improvement initiatives since the industrial age began. Every company struggles in an increasingly competitive market and many attempt to reduce costs by trying to involve their employees. Some efforts succeed, but many don't.

Why do so many of these efforts fail? A major contributing factor is that management has difficulty finding the appropriate ways to interact with their employees. It is simply easier to try, and possibly fail without involving the workforce, than it is to do the things necessary to involve them and insure success.

Another factor is that some managers approach solutions

to problems because they want to be the hero. Solving big problems means career success. The problem with this approach is that most managers aren't close enough to the work to understand what the best solution is. That causes resentment among those who do understand the work.

To continually improve, you have to understand that you must have help from others. To gain the interest of your employees you must answer that basic question that is most important to all of us, "What's in it for me?" Though it may seem selfish, this is everyone's first reaction to new programs. If a new improvement program is rolled out by management and it involves filling out new reports or completing additional tasks, aren't you going to wonder where you are going to find time to get these new reports filled out and complete these new tasks, and still do the rest of the things you already do? When a new program is rolled out, has anyone ever added, "and by the way, just forget about doing those old reports?" It almost never happens that way. If the answer to the "What's in it for me?" question is perceived to be additional work for you and credit for someone else, we're all bound to react negatively and fight the change.

On the flip side, if you approach a change initiative understanding that first you need to address the employee's needs by showing how the new program saves them time or makes their job easier or makes the job more satisfying, you are more likely to get the employee's cooperation, which will, in turn, increase the chance for success of the new program or system.

Most front-line supervisors are better at involving their employees than upper or middle managers because they better understand the need for employee satisfaction.

Generally, the first reaction you get from a front-line supervisor after sitting through a multi-hour session explaining the importance of employee buy-in is "I already do that!" The problem is, however, front-line supervisors rarely have time to work on long-term, forward-looking system improvements.

Consulting companies who specialize in improvement initiatives suggest that you involve your employees more and recommend building teams. However, how you set these teams up is critical. This is how failed team building efforts usually progress:

- First, employees are separated into teams.
- Next, the teams have meetings to "brainstorm" ideas and build lists.
- Then, upper management has a meeting to prioritize the ideas on the lists.
- Sometimes, ideas are run past accountants to validate the estimated savings.
- Then, management passes the list back down the management chain so each level can have meetings on how to implement.
- Then, the lists are given to the front-line supervisors to get things done. (What's in it for them? More work.)

This approach is the epitome of the inefficient batch processing observed by the "Lean Thinkers." By the time employees and front-line supervisors get through the process they are tired of having meetings, building lists and getting nowhere. They just want to find a way to make it all stop so they can go do some "real work." As time progresses communication falters, employees hear nothing about the status of their ideas, and begin to understand their input didn't matter and that it was all a waste of time.

Effective Employee Participation

What's the solution? In an article written by Paul R. Lawrence for the *Harvard Business Review* in May—June, 1954 that reviewed research that dealt with employee participation, Mr. Lawrence enumerated the findings of a study that was done by Lester Coch and John R.P. French, Jr.[27] that looked at three different types of employee participation and their impact on affecting change.

The first group was a "No Participation" group where a change was introduced by engineering staff members holding a meeting with the employees and informing them of the change that was to occur. The employees were then sent back to the factory floor with work instructions to implement the change.

The second group was a "Participation through Representation" group. Change was introduced by engineering staff members who held meetings with representatives of the workforce to supply their input for new ideas and to communicate progress to the workforce.

The third group was a "Total Participation" group. Here, engineering staff members met with all of the workers and explained the change and asked them for their input in implementing the change. The groups then discussed how improvements could be made and how wasteful steps could be eliminated.

In both the "No Participation" group and the "Participation by Representation" group, a dramatic reduction in productivity was experienced due to hostility toward staff members and resistance to change. The top down approach caused resentment and employees generally found ways to make sure the new approach did not work. In the "Participation by Representation" group the temporary drop in productivity was eventually reversed. The "Total Participation" group experienced a less dramatic decrease in productivity and rebounded to higher productivity levels. Unlike the others, in this group "there were no signs of hostility toward the staff people or toward the supervisors, and there were no quits during the experimental period."[28] Coch and French concluded that the resistance seen was not so much to a "technical change, but rather resistance to social or human changes that often accompany technical innovations." [29]

The following excerpt details Lawrence's theory that resistance to technical change is unnecessary if managers and supervisors begin to think about their employees in a different way. Here are the five points Lawrence states in his article:

"1. A solution which has become increasingly popular for dealing with resistance to change is to get the people involved to "participate" in making the change. But as a practical matter "participation" as a device is not a good way for management to think about the problem. In fact, it may lead to trouble.

2. The key to the problem is to understand the true nature of resistance. Actually, what employees resist is usually not technical change but social change— the change in their human relationships that generally accompanies technical change.

3. Resistance is usually created because of certain blind spots and attitudes, which staff specialists have as a

result of their preoccupation with the technical aspects of new ideas.

4. Management can take concrete steps to deal constructively with these staff attitudes. The steps include emphasizing new standards of performance for staff specialists and encouraging them to think in different ways, as well as making use of the fact that signs of resistance can serve as a practical warning signal in directing and timing technological changes.

5. Top executives can also make their own efforts more effective at meetings of staff and operating groups where change is being discussed. They can do this by shifting their attention from the facts of schedules, technical details, work assignments, and so forth, to what the discussion of these terms indicates in regard to developing resistance and receptiveness to change." [30]

During studies in another plant, Lawrence watched a staff member who was interacting with an operator in the field and observed that a social connection was made. In this instance dramatic technical changes were implemented.

He also observed a staff member who simply directed operators to make technical changes. After a failed attempt to implement the technical change the operator turned to the engineer and, with a triumphant air, said, "It doesn't work."

Lawrence's conclusion: "Participation will never work so long as it is treated as a device to get other people to do what you want them to. Real participation is based on respect. And respect is not acquired by just trying; it is acquired when the staff people face the reality that they need the contributions of the operating people." [31]

To get that cooperation, managers need to concentrate first on answering the basic human question "What's in this for me?" understanding that the most effective way to do that is one-on-one interaction. The rest of the implementation process becomes much easier, and more permanent, once social barriers are eliminated and replaced with social connections.

From these works we can categorize four methods of employee participation, in ascending order of effectiveness:

- No Employee Participation
- Employee Participation by Representation
- Full Employee Participation
- One-on-One Employee Interaction

Of these, One-on-One Employee Interaction netted the highest sustainable productivity gains while experiencing the least amount of resistance to technical change.

Processing Employee Ideas

While the most effective method of employee participation is "One-on-One Interaction," it is sometimes impractical to get everyone's ideas one person at a time. Sometimes you have to have meetings with large groups of employees.

In the consulting scenario described at the beginning of this chapter, several bureaucratic steps were added to the process before any implementation efforts were made.

Generally, when lists are generated from group meetings the process becomes an entity unto itself and can overrun the original idea of implementing improvements. The process becomes so involved that any desired savings are offset by the cost of the bureaucracy to support the process.

The most economical way to process employee ideas is to make sure that the group understands that you are meeting to come up with new ways, which the group can control, to improve the process. Next, each group needs to process ideas on a "first in, first out" basis. Avoid large lists which make it harder to prioritize and manage, thereby making it harder to complete all of the items on the list. It's critical to remember that soliciting an employee's ideas and then failing to act on them is worse than never asking at all.

Processing ideas should be handled similar to processing materials, as described by "Lean Thinkers" Womack and Jones. They recommend that all production systems eliminate any form of batch processing and move toward a system of continuous flow. Batch processing builds in the overhead costs of re-handling ideas, while continuous flow processing helps eliminate many levels of bureaucratic waste.

In short, this means no lists and no approvals. Instead, as employees bring their ideas forward, employees, supervisors and managers should be empowered to work together to evaluate ideas, prioritize them, and then to act on them. This ensures strong employee acceptance and improvements that can be made quickly without suffocating bureaucracy. Employees see quicker results and companies see greater benefits, which promote future input and continuous improvement.

Individual Participation on Teams

As leaders, we generally want to lead, but is it good to always assume we know best? Because we are in the position we are in, we usually have a very good chance for success using only our own ideas and drive to accomplish the mission at hand. If we want to improve faster, however, we need to be creative in finding ways to solicit and incorporate the ideas of others into continuous improvement plans.

To accomplish this, however, we have to learn to park our egos. Many people use "team" as a regular part of their vocabulary, but few people actually understand the meaning of the word. The effective manager understands team. The effective manager is that individual who not only has good ideas on how to do things, but who is also able to listen to the ideas of others and incorporate the better parts of everyone's ideas.

Types of Individual Participation

There are four types of employee participation used in team meetings, each indicating certain management tendencies:

Non-participation—Non-participation may indicate the employee feels intimidated by others in the group or is uncomfortable verbalizing their ideas. This individual may want to be led by others.

Passive participation—Passive participants are usually willing to participate if asked but are otherwise quiet. Typically, they listen attentively but may not feel comfortable leading. They quickly stop contributing when challenged.

Active participation—Active participants are comfortable leading others. They actively suggest ideas but also understand they need to solicit the ideas of others and are good at making others feel they are part of the group, soliciting their ideas and incorporating those ideas into the plan.

Dominant participation—The dominant participant insists on being in control. They are not interested in soliciting the input of others or listening to their ideas, but rather, are more interested in directing the group toward their own solution to a problem, one they believe to be the only solution. This person is a "command and control" junkie.

No one type of team participation style is correct for every situation. In one meeting it may be appropriate to minimize your participation to promote the ideas of others, while in another situation it may be necessary to dictate the direction for the team by dominating the meeting. Generally, however, effective managers are active participants who enthusiastically get things moving by suggesting ideas and are not threatened by the input of others. They are good at taking in ideas from each team member and helping the group build a team solution.

Employee Reward Systems

Managers sometimes try to find reward systems that will help them motivate their employees and keep them happy. Motivating employees and keeping them happy, however, is the job of good supervisors. Rewards systems should be used to recognize and promote the behaviors you want to see your employees exhibit and not used as a crutch because supervisors don't have the leadership skills they need to adequately fulfill their role as motivational leaders.

One problem with paying for achievement is that too soon after an employee begins to receive performance rewards, they begin to feel that these rewards are owed to them for their usual duties. Once they subconsciously begin to feel that a regular days work deserves special recognition and reward, they begin to expect the reward all of the time and the reward loses it's meaning. Just ask anyone who has ever had to "undo" an out of control reward system.

Workable Rewards Systems

Rewards systems are only workable if they are designed so that everyone has the opportunity to achieve the reward. There are several types of workable rewards systems that do reward behavior that will help keep productivity and longevity fresh in people's minds. A couple of examples are bonus for years of service and bonus for profitability.

Bonus Based on Longevity—Bonus based on years of service is an effective way to promote employee longevity in a strong job market. Systems based on five, ten, fifteen and twenty years put monies out in front of employees that they must consider losing if other job opportunities arise. A bonus for years of service system puts money away for the future, for each day the employee is employed. Longevity systems are similar to 401K programs, where pulling out early results in financial penalties. Sticking with a company over the long run means your money continues to grow and results in a payoff for your years of investment in the company.

A typically example of bonus for longevity is $5,000 (or

some portion or multiple) for five years, $10,000 for ten years, $15,000 for fifteen years, etc. In these types of bonus systems employees have an investment decision, as well as a short-term monetary decision, when considering alternate job options.

The other benefit to the longevity system is that the capital for the payouts is earned over time and is placed in interest earning accounts. If $.50 is put into an investment fund for every employee hour worked, the money is building earnings for the company while the employee is contributing his years of service. If the employee leaves early, the principal investment as well as the investment earnings, belong to the company.

Bonus Based on Profitability—Bonus based on number of units sold, or cash flow into the organization, is a good way to tie the success of the employees to the success of the company by keeping productivity and sales as a priority for them.

Bonus for profitability must be tied, however, to cash realized by the company and not just production of units. It won't do a company any good if they produce, and pay bonus on, a number of units that can't be sold in a difficult market. Tying employees as a group to the sale of the product encourages employees to become ad hoc members of the company's sales team. Setting this bonus up as a group reward can also eliminate the possible damage caused by some types of competition.

Outstanding Achievement Awards

Extreme caution should be given before starting any outstanding achievement reward program. Outstanding achievement awards should only be used when the desired performance target is truly outstanding and determined well in advance, so that all have the same opportunity to strive for the achievement.

Most times outstanding achievement awards do more harm than good. Typically, the supervisor is asked, or decides, to put someone in his department up for nomination as an outstanding employee. The supervisor, without any clear guidelines, picks that person who *seems* to be the best person in the group. The supervisor usually picks someone he can usually count on to get the job done and be cooperative toward the group's goals. Yet, what is the upside potential for the company? The person you selected is already a hardworking, motivated individual. They already put everything "on the line" for you. What more is there for them to give?

On the flip side, there are a lot of hardworking people on a crew who won't get recognized. The employees who didn't get recognized begin to question why they didn't get recognized. Dissension begins to creep into your workforce and they may begin to believe that the buddy system is in play. Unrecognized employees can, and will, recite every time they have ever worked as hard, or harder, than the person who got the award. This leads them to become sour toward the supervisor and the company.

Then there are the unmotivated few that you are trying to motivate by recognizing the appropriate behavior. Sorry. Nothing works for them except constant supervision.

As time goes on, the person who was recognized gets so much flack from others in the department about getting the recognition, they soon make it clear not to consider them in the future. Those who didn't receive it for comparable contributions become bitter and the slackers sit back and enjoy the dissension.

Who wins? No one. Not the employee who was recognized, not the other hardworking employees in the department, and especially not the company, whose original goal was to motivate the workforce to be more productive.

Management groups should exercise caution when selecting employee rewards systems. The cost to benefit ratio can be questionable, and the hidden costs of de-motivating others can be substantial.

However, it is still important to reward employees by praising them and tapping into their pride. Remember not to underestimate the power of your employee's desire to please those in authority. Tapping into this employee resource is a big part of what you should be providing for your company.

Conclusion

Supervision is like any other craft. While you never fully master it, your mission should be to continually strive to improve your skills and reach the next level of effectiveness. When you reach that level, go to the next, constantly pushing outward into the new frontiers of supervision.[32] While traveling on the journey of supervision, being responsible for everything under the sun, including the company's resources, your employee's well-being, and the success or failure of both, you'll find it a heavy burden to bear. Those who enjoy challenges, however, will find the work rewarding and fulfilling.

As you achieve success and recognition for your efforts, don't forget your responsibility to those coming up. You learned your skills, and became what you are, with the help of those who were willing to teach and mentor you. It is incumbent upon you to pass that knowledge and experience along to each succeeding generation, so that the craft of supervision can continue to grow, and so each company, and its employees, are better able to reach their potential.

Failure to live up to this responsibility means a slide backwards for supervisors of the future, which will result in weaker companies and many more unproductive and unhappy employees than is acceptable. Meeting your responsibility will result in a tremendous feeling of satisfaction in knowing that you were able to influence future generations to be more than they might have otherwise been.

Remember how important it is to enjoy yourself while supervising, because a job without satisfaction will only provide financial reward, and will not satisfy your deeper need to take pride in your work and feel your efforts are beneficial.

Finally, never assume you have reached your final destination, for there is only the journey, and the pride in knowing that you were one of those chosen to make the trip.

Planning for Improved Performance

"The aim of leadership should be to improve the performance of man and machine, to improve quality, to increase output, and simultaneously to bring pride of workmanship to people." Dr. W. Edwards Deming [33]

As supervisors, it is our responsibility to reject the status quo and to make the effort to continually improve. Just as you must make the commitment to improve, you must also build an action plan for moving forward.

Take the following steps to develop an outline for an Improvement Action Plan.

1. Determine which areas you would like to improve in.
2. Develop an action plan that outlines the keys steps you need to take.
3. Take action.

Which areas do I want to improve in?

1.
2.
3.
4.

Improvement Action Plan Outline:

I. Why is it important to improve?

    A.
    B.

II. What do I think is important to accomplish?

    A.
    B.

III. What are the barriers that might exist that could prevent my improvement?

    A.
    B.

IV. What actions will I take to insure success?

    A.

    B.

Bibliography of References

[1] As of the date of this printing, Newmont Mining had become the largest gold mining producer in the world.

[2] Main points taken from *Effective Foremanship*, (National Electrical Contractors Association—1969), page 4. Original descriptions have been modified, updated or paraphrased.

[3] International Loss Control Institute—1989

[4] *Effective Foremanship*, (National Electrical Contractors Association—1969), Foreword. Original descriptions have been modified, updated or paraphrased.

[5] Ibid., page 5. See note above. Numbers six and seven have been added to this list.

[6] Ibid., pages 6 and 7. See note above.

[7] Robert Wilson, *Maintenance Technology Magazine*, October 2000 (Applied Technology Publications, Inc.—2000)

[8] The Supervisor's Effectiveness Rating Graph does not represent statistical data, but rather the author's opinion based on his own experiences.

[9] *Effective Foremanship*, (National Electrical Contractors Association—1969), page 25. Original descriptions have been modified, updated or paraphrased.

[10] Ibid., page 29.

[11] David M. Potter as quoted by James M. McPherson, "How Lincoln Won the War with Metaphor," contained

in *With My Face to the Enemy: Perspectives on the Civil War*, page 8, (G.P. Putnam's Sons—2001)

12 James M. McPherson, "How Lincoln Won the War with Metaphor," contained in *With My Face to the Enemy: Perspectives on the Civil War*, page 8, (G.P. Putnam's Sons—2001)

13 Ibid

14 Paul D. Escott, as quoted by James M. McPherson, "How Lincoln Won the War with Metaphor," contained in *With My Face to the Enemy: Perspectives on the Civil War*, page 8, (G.P. Putnam's Sons—2001)

15 John Bartlett, *Bartlett's Familiar Quotations,* edited for the 16th Edition by Justin Caplan, (Little, Brown and Company—1992)

16 Michael Mauser, Ph.D., from a group session on improving speaking skills - 2001

17 Quoted from a Toastmaster's speech given by Gil Sargent in August of 2000.

18 Michael Mauser, Ph.D., see note 16.

19 Quoted from a conversation with Doug Jones, Underground Mine Manager - 1999

20 E.L. Thorndike and Clarence L. Barnhart, *Thorndike Barnhart—Fifth Edition Dictionary*, (Scott, Foresman and Company—1964)

21 Author unknown

22 *Effective Foremanship*, (National Electrical Contractors Association—1969) page 12.

23 Ibid., pages 14 and 15. See note above.

24 James P. Womack and Daniel T. Jones, *Lean Thinking*, (Simon and Schuster—1996) Notes page 313, quoting from Taiichi Ohno, *The Toyota Production System: Beyond*

Large Scale Production (Productivity Press, Portland, Oregon, 1988) pages 19-20.

25 Ibid., page 313.

26 Ibid., page 50-52.

27 Lester Coch and John R.P. French, Jr., *Overcoming Resistance to Change, Human Relations, Vol. 1, No. 4,* 1948, page 512.

28 Paul R. Lawrence, *How to Deal with Resistance to Change* (HBR Classic, May-June, 1954), reprint order number 68107

29 Coch and French, *Overcoming Resistance to Change, Human Relations,* page 512.

30 Lawrence, *How to Deal with Resistance to Change*

31 Ibid.

32 These new frontiers of supervision are those skills, and that base of knowledge and strategies, that are new to you as a supervisor and open for your exploration. Most of the information has been around for years and is known, and has been written about by many.

33 W. Edwards Deming, *Out of Crisis,* (Massachusetts Institute of Technology, Center for Advanced Engineering Study—1986), excerpted by Rafael Aguayuo, *Dr. Deming, The Man Who Taught the Japanese About Quality,* (Simon and Schuster—1990)

Recommended Reading

There are many books that can help you understand how to successfully supervise employees and manage departments. Here is a list of a few of the books and articles that I recommend for increasing your knowledge, and improving your skills as a supervisor.

Effective Foremanship, (National Electrical Contractors Association—1969)

The Machine that Changed the World, James P. Womack, Daniel T. Jones, and Daniel Roos, (Harpers Perennial—1990)

Lean Thinking, James P. Womack and Daniel T. Jones, (Simon and Schuster—1996)

How to Deal with Resistance to Change, Paul R. Lawrence, (HBR Classic, May-June 1954 - Reprint Order Number 68107)

From Worst to First, Gordon Bethune with Scott Huler, (John Wiley and Sons—1998)

Out of Crisis, W. Edwards Deming (Massachusetts Institute of Technology, Center for Advanced Engineering Study—1986)

Dr. Deming, The Man Who Taught the Japanese About Quality, Rafael Aguayuo, (Simon and Schuster—1990)

The Mask of Command, John Keegan (Penguin Books—1987)